ProspHER(ish

The diary of a fcuked up female ...

Author, Serena Fordham, is the founder of ProspHER - educating and empowering women to achieve their professional aspirations, to fulfil their true potential and live the lives they dream of.

ProspHER*(ish)* contains raw and real-life accounts of Serena's fragile journey, while navigating the turbulent world of building a successful business.

Written and Cover Design by Serena Fordham from ProspHER.

In memory of two beautiful souls in heaven: Sonia Catchpole (auntie) and Monica Payne (grandma).

First Published 2024 by Serena Fordham

This Edition Published 2024 by Serena Fordham

72 Godfrey Road, Spixworth, Norwich, NR10 3NL

ISBN: 979-8-33-203510-4

Written in Norwich, Norfolk, England.

Foreword - Following the breadcrumbs

Written by Katie Oman

Do you believe in synchronicity?

I certainly do. I have been shown time and time again that there's magic in the Universe and, when we follow the breadcrumbs laid out before us, we can go on totally unforeseen but wonderful adventures.

I had one of those magic moments in September 2022.

After the summer holidays, I was randomly invited by the head of the charity Hopestead to attend a talk for free in the city *(Breadcrumb Number 1)*.

After having my twins for six weeks, I was desperate to do something that was just for me, and I jumped at the opportunity.

This talk was given by Dr. Sam Collins, who is the CEO of the women's training and coaching company, Aspire. She had written a book called *Rebellious* and was talking about how we can all show up in our lives and careers in ways that weren't small and playing it safe - but would take things bigger.

During this talk, she had us up and talking to each other (you could feel the awkwardness in a room of British people at this!) We had to go and tell someone about our big, scary dream. I went over to one of the few men in the room and asked him this. *"I don't know..."* he muttered, so I helped him figure out his first (what can I say? - once a coach, always a coach!) When he asked me what mine was, I told him that I wanted to open a centre for women. A place of education, support and empowerment. A real safe space for women to come together.

"Women don't need safe spaces".

Yes, he actually said this - and no, I didn't kill him (though I was tempted).

Once the event was over, that thought wouldn't leave my mind and, me being the woman I am, I raced home to jump on the computer. Typing into Google, *Women's*

Centres UK, I emailed as many as I could, asking for advice to help me make this dream a reality.

Out of all the ones I emailed, one got back to me. It was a charity based in Liverpool of all places...which is where I'm originally from *(Breadcrumb Number 2)*.

They pointed me back to Norfolk and the New Anglia Growth Hub, which supports people in business. After chatting with them about my own business, I received an email two weeks later...

'There's this event happening at The Forum today, which I think would be great for you. It's probably short notice, but it's worth a look" (Breadcrumb Number 3).

It was short notice as I had client calls, so I emailed the woman running it and introduced myself, thinking it could lead to a speaking opportunity or something. Two hours later, I received an email back...

"This woman has left the company, but I want to talk to you".

That email was sent by none other than Serena. A woman with whom I'd been friends with three years previously, but with whom I'd lost touch with!

We jumped onto a Zoom call and chatted away about life, kids, and ProspHER. She told me all about her amazing company, and I instantly knew that I had to be involved. As a women's empowerment coach myself, supporting and uplifting women is both my passion and my purpose. Hearing how ProspHER has the intention of "Passion, Purpose and Power" for women, and that Serena wants to support at least a million women by 2030, I knew that our paths were totally aligned. Getting onboard was a total no-brainer!

Since then, I have gone on to be the Events Manager for ProspHER Fest Norwich in September 2023. This was a phenomenal event that saw around 250 women and their families attend for a day of connection, education, laughter and support. I have since gone on to become the Events Director of ProspHER, where I support other Event Managers to make their events incredible for both themselves and the people who attend them.

The synchronicities that led me to ProspHER are ones that I am so deeply thankful for. Following those breadcrumbs was one of the best things that I ever did; even if I couldn't understand where I was being led at the time!

ProspHER is a company that continues to grow and develop, and I know that we will meet all of our goals and intentions. In fact, not only will we meet them, but we will surpass them, too!

Yes, there have been more ups and downs than the world's biggest roller coaster on this journey, but I have seen what happens when you have an inspirational and caring person at the helm. Serena is a wonderful leader to work with, and I feel blessed to walk this path with her. I have absolutely no doubts at all that the future looks bright.

Truly, we will "ProspHER" with "Passion, Purpose and Power!"

Love and hugs,
Katie xx

Katie Oman is the Events Director at ProspHER. Alongside this, she also has her own business, working as a women's empowerment coach, motivational speaker and event organiser. Katie is an author of nine books so far, and she is a book coach who helps others to write and publish their own books. To date, she has helped fifteen incredible women to do just that, including an Amazon bestseller and an award-winning children's book.

To find out more about her, go to www.katieoman.co.uk.

The Greatest Show: Me and Serena at the entrance of ProspHER Fest Norwich in September 2023.

Chapter 1 - Beginning with the end

I have a confession to make.

This book originally started out with the title *ProspHERous*, and as a sequel to my previous Amazon bestselling business book *HER Funny Business*, was supposed to focus on all the incredible progress and success I had achieved between one book to the next.

You know, to inspire all you readers to feel that you yourselves can achieve huge success in business too, and in fact, whatever you want to achieve in your life.

However, it has ended up being named *ProspHER(ish)*, because life never goes to plan. In early 2024 my life turned upside down when I had major surgery (more on that later) that led me on a different road. So, even though I have "ProspHERed" (sorry, I had to!) between writing my last book and this one, I've had lots of ups and downs along the way and have made some mistakes throughout the journey!

So, I wouldn't consider myself "ProspHERous" just yet - although do we ever really get there? After all, we are always developing and evolving, aren't we? Life and business is a continuous journey and there's never a final destination!

For those who have read my previous book - you can skip the next bit as you are completely up-to-date on my story. But, for those that haven't yet (psst, you might want to head to Amazon to order and read it first for context) - I will give you the low-down in a brief summary.

I graduated from my Business Management degree in 2009. During that time the recession was in full swing and I had applied for hundreds of jobs in the desperate attempt to find employment. By accident, I fell into a role within Estate Agency, but secretly hated it due to the harsh competitiveness and tough sales targets.

Even though I thrived in the role, due to it being people-focused and was promoted quickly, I never really had any love for it. Plus, the pressure to lie to customers, the extremely long and unsociable hours, and the fake nature of flashy company cars, but low base salary, all didn't align with my values.

In 2011, I found out my (then) husband was cheating on me, which led to a messy divorce, and an even messier Serena (both mentally and physically, as I was exhausted, living on 10 cans of Redbull a day and battling an eating disorder).

In the same year, my life transformed dramatically and, fast-forward to the end of 2011, I had met my (now) husband, Matthew, and was pregnant with my first born.

Life was incredible, or so I portrayed it to be. I gave birth to a healthy baby girl after a longgggggg six day labour in September 2012, but maternity leave was a struggle as I had always worked. I had completely lost part of my identity, and struggled with postnatal depression, which developed into full on manic depression and thoughts of suicide.

Mentally, I was on a roller-coaster, but I still plodded on with the menial tasks of life - continuously clock-watching and counting down the hours, minutes and seconds until I would have adult company again.

The thought of going back to work in late 2013 was also filling me with dread. I was struggling with motherhood, but also hated my worklife in Property Management. I was left feeling useless and completely lost about where I was heading in life.

In the Summer of 2013, while planning mine and Matthew's wedding for November 2013, I was made redundant from my role as Lettings Manager - finding out in an email that I had been accidentally CC'd into by my boss to his solicitor. At the time my heart sank, as money was already tight and we were relying on me going back to work to be able to pay for our wedding.

Worry turned into relief as I decided at that point I was going to do what I'd always wanted to do - start my own business. So, in order to help my husband put food on the table for our growing family (which was expensive as my first born, Ella, loved to eat!) I set up my first business; Glow Virtual Assistants. This meant I was able to work flexibly around caring for my daughter and earn independently, while also doing things I was passionate about (communicating with people, organising, and business).

With my qualifications and experience working in various sales and marketing roles while at uni, I soon found my flow and got into the swing of juggling motherhood and self-employment like a mother-fcuking boss! I built a team and grew the business mainly through client referrals and word of mouth. But, I still felt something was missing.

The missing piece was that all Glow's clients were men! So, when I began working with a social media marketing woman who asked me to help her with the admin for a local business women's networking group I jumped at the chance. Then, in 2015, this client became too busy and asked me to take over the group. How could I refuse?!

HER Business Revolution, as it eventually became, grew quicker than I thought and soon was larger than Glow had ever been - meaning I decided to sell the Virtual

Assistants business in 2018 to focus on my main passion of helping women in business succeed.

2019 was a big year for HBR. As well as me releasing my *HER Funny Business* book, our networking groups, conferences, workshops and retreats were expanding across the UK and our online membership was beginning to take off.

That's my summary. I hope you've fully caught up now.

"What exciting things happened next?" I hear you ask.

Well, the Covid-19 pandemic hit in March 2020, everyone locked down and many businesses came to a standstill (including mine!)

But, the pandemic was the best thing that could have happened, and afterwards from the ashes of HER Business Revolution rose ProspHER*(ish)*.

My Model Pose: Me unleashing my "inner model" in a ProspHER photoshoot, at our office in June 2022.

Chapter 2 - The shit show became a circus

I blinked and the strange mixture of chaos and calm that came from the pandemic passed, and all the conversations I'd had virtually with women over the past year had led me to the point where I realised that my company could no longer just focus on supporting women who had set up their own businesses because so many were transitioning into employment in the corporate world.

It became clear that Covid-19 hadn't just caused negative health and social impacts, but it had completely changed the whole landscape of work.

ProspHER had to widen it's net and include even more women, no matter what their role or aspirations. So, the small employed team of seven at the time set to work on rebranding the business, redesigning the website and launching a completely new event that encompassed work, mindset and wellbeing.

May 2022 saw the first one of its kind hosted in Norwich, and from the outside, ProspHER was thriving and it seemed that I was excelling as a founder too. But, nothing is ever as it seems, hey?

At this time, I was living the life and running the business I had always dreamed of. Driving an Audi A4 (my childhood dream car), I employed people, we worked in a fancy office and we were a profitable company. Slick and shiny. The big issue was, I had made myself ill - both physically and mentally.

You see, my diet was horrendous and I had been working all the waking hours I could, meaning that I wasn't sleeping properly, I was quickly gaining weight and I wasn't spending any quality time with my husband and two kids. Living this lifestyle for the past year since emerging from the last lockdown had taken its toll on my mind and body. I was absolutely exhausted and ProspHER - and the heavy load that came with it - was sucking out my soul, to the point that I didn't recognise who I was becoming.

In early 2022 I had been diagnosed with Type Two Diabetes, which had nudged me into making some slight changes to better look after myself, but it wasn't enough.

The growing stress I had put on my body had built up to the point that this illness was taking a hold of me, and paired with my IBS (Irritable Bowel Syndrome) - which had flared its ugly head often since I developed "Delhi Belly" (i.e. food poisoning) from a uni trip to India back in 2009 - caused me to be sicker than I has ever been before.

Moving into a new office in March 2022 was enough to elevate my symptoms to a completely new level. Vomiting, diarrhoea, sweats, tremors, migraines, blurry vision and passing out were daily occurrences, and meant that I was bed-ridden by the time our first SUPERWOMAN Fest took place.

As a female-founder, my business meant a lot to me. But, being severely ill and feeling I couldn't talk to anyone about it (because of the underlying fear that if I did then people would see me as a failure), sent my mind into complete self-destruct mode. I began to feel jealous of my team members for being the "face" of the company, when I was the one doing all the difficult work behind the scenes - and getting none of the glory for it. I felt frustrated that our Managing Director was centre-stage at our events, talking to all our customers, mingling with all the company contacts I had built up, and taking all the praise for the successful business that ProspHER was becoming.

This feeling of FOMO (Fear Of Missing Out) clouded my judgement. After the first festival, this feeling of jealousy made me erratic. I was making snap decisions and confusing the whole team. I was changing things for the sake of making changes. I was arguing with the MD on a daily basis. All in the desperate attempt to show my dominance and claw back some control over the company I had founded seven years before.

And, as a result, things started to go downhill quickly.

Myself and the team were in the process of planning the next SUPERWOMAN Fest event (again in Norwich, where I'm based) for October 2022. But, as swift changes and toxicity between the team was at an all time high - partly due to my negative mental state and physical absence from the business, and partly due to the nastiness and unsporting nature of one particular employee (who I had wrongfully promoted by that point to step into my role while I was unwell) - staff began to leave, workload piled up and income tried up completely.

I had taken a part-time business lecturing role at my local college (which was due to begin in September) in the attempt to attract some income to keep my years of hard work afloat during this tough period. But, as we headed towards the second festival, it became clear that big changes were needed if ProspHER was to have any kind of shot at a future.

With my mindset and mental state steadily improving with plenty of rest, journaling, meditation and time with my family, in the attempt to stay in control of the struggling situation, I set the team we had left some minimal income targets and easily achievable KPIs (Key Performance Indicators) to get things back on track.

I had been studying effective communication in the Level Seven Strategic Management and Leadership Apprenticeship I had additionally been working on at the time (which instead of adding additional stress, actually helped me focus and give me clarity about the future direction of the company) - so was confident of my approach in sharing these targets with the team and being completely candid and clear in my reasons to encourage understanding in a positive way.

I was met with reactions of pure disgust from the team. I think because I had not displayed this type of leadership dominance, and in honesty had trusted the employees to do what was best for the business until then, these targets were not well received.

I remember having a long conversation with my "stand-in" (aka our MD) during August 2022 (whom at that point seemed to do the complete opposite of everything I suggested to be awkward because apparently, even though I had studied business management and strategy since high school and had run/sold another successful company in the past, I *"had no idea what I was talking about"* - her words). During this phone call there was just blame for not coming even close to the KPIs set - all aimed in my direction.

Nevermind that I hadn't been able to be at the forefront of the business to build relationships and make sales.

Regardless that I had taken an additional job, so I didn't need to take personal income from the business. Ignoring the fact that I had said *"yes"* to every single thing this member of staff had requested - *"we need an office"*, *"I need a company car"*, *"my expenses need to be paid to attend these networking events"* - *"yes, yes, yes"*. I never had any objections.

But, in that moment when I was being screamed at down the phone that everything that had gone wrong in the last year was my fault, the word *"no"* was the only one on the tip of my tongue.

Enough was enough.

ProspHER had turned into a circus.

This other employee was the only one left. No one else could work with her. She was unprofessional, rude, unorganised and selfish. She didn't care about anyone else but herself - and I finally could see it.

On that call I cried, hung up several times and unleashed my anger. I couldn't take the disrespect, bullying and drama any longer.

I gave notice on the office because we couldn't afford it (and no longer needed it). We packed up our stuff and moved out separately because we were hardly talking to one another. I was still physically unwell and undergoing loads of tests because of the issues I was having with my stomach - even at one point facing a cancer diagnosis (which was super scary) - but I still went through the motions of doing what I needed to do for ProspHER that month leading up to the October event.

As myself and the MD were working independently and along different tangents at this time, I was unwise to what would happen next.

Regardless of her toxic traits, I never thought she would stoop as low as she did.

One morning, only weeks before the sequel to our first ProspHER-branded event, I sent an email to give this person notice of reduced hours that we would have to gravitate to once the next festival had taken place. I didn't want to, but the only way the company could survive financially was to reduce another expense, and as we were paying through the nose for her company car, cutting down our hours was the only viable option.

Less than an hour after sending this email and receiving her agreeing response, I received an email from Eventbrite saying that the login details to this system had been changed. My first thought was this could be a mistake or a scam, so I attempted to login to regain access.

Luckily, as I'm pretty tech savvy, I managed to get into the account within a few minutes, and after searching around Eventbrite to check nothing savage had happened as a result of this glitch, I made an eye-opening discovery. My one and only member of staff had taken it upon herself to login and change the payout bank account details from the company bank account to her own personal bank account. As you can imagine, attempted theft of company income wasn't an act that aligned well with my values.

This was the straw that broke the camel's back.

I had trusted this person. We had once had a great working relationship. She was the obvious choice to be promoted and take over some of my role when I was unwell. I once had no issue with fulfilling her request of increasing her hours, setting her up in an office and giving her a brand new company car, because I thought that (like me) she cared about the company.

But, staring in disbelief at her misplaced bank details, the glimmer of trust and respect that I was left with withered away in that second.

I was furious.

Ok, so what I did next probably wasn't the best way to have handled the situation - but bear in mind that since early 2022 I had been very ill and my head had been all over the place.

So, I messaged her asking her if she had changed the login details on the Eventbrite account. No answer.

I waited a few minutes, then messaged her to say I knew it was her that had changed the login information as the username had been set as her email address. She responded:

"I just don't trust you!"

The phrase *"the pot calling the kettle black"* sprang to mind!

I was even more angry.

Then I messaged her to say that I had discovered that she had changed the bank account details so the payout from the event taking place in a week-or-so's time would get sent to her.

She didn't see anything wrong with her actions.

I was confused.

Have you not heard of misconduct?

I knew in my heart right then that this person had to go.

I restricted her access to all ProspHER's systems and agreed with her that I would send her all the information she needed to host the event as planned. She agreed in writing that it was the right decision.

So, the event was happening in early October as planned (well apart from being branded towards this woman as a "one-person-show", with no mention of the company!) But, I let that go, thinking she would return her company car as agreed after the event and we could part ways amicably.

I couldn't have been more wrong*(ish)*.

Wearing My Mask: Me and my mum at the theatre on the night before the SUPERWOMAN Fest October 2022

(I was smiling on the outside, but a mess on the inside).

Chapter 3 - Into the black hole

What a roller-coaster of a year 2022 had already been. My personal life was a mess, my professional life was hanging by a thread.

Thankfully I was still pushing on with my apprenticeship, and my monthly calls with my Tutor and coach, Helen, were really helping me to gain perspective and make informed decisions based on my intuition and knowledge gained from the learning modules.

After the second SUPERWOMAN Fest, of which during that day I had to switch off from the world of social media and retreat to Cromer, a seaside town, with my biggest cheerleader and loyal therapist (aka my mum), the company car wasn't returned to my driveway as expected.

I felt a mixture of surprise and disappointment, but still giving the benefit of the doubt to this person who had deliberately intended to screw me over, I sent a polite and professional email.

Only to receive an instant reply to say that if I wanted the car back I'd have to go to her driveway and get it.

I wasn't in the right headspace for any kind of confrontation. I wanted a black hole to swallow me up. I didn't even want to interact with the world, let alone walk into the lion's den!

I called the police to find out if there was anything I could do, but they said it was a civil dispute and said there was nothing that could be done to get the company's property back. I felt so lost and completely defeated. Why was this person making this situation even worse by digging her heels in?

Behind closed doors I referred to her as "the Evil Queen" from then on, as the way she was acting had stripped away her fake mask and revealed her true devious self.

After emailing back and forth (and receiving some really nasty threats) I stuck to my guns and the agreement we had made a few weeks prior, and the car was finally returned to the curb outside my house late one night a few days after the event. I held my breath as I looked around it for damage in the light the next morning.

Phew, it was unharmed.

The car lease people came to collect it that day and as they drove it away a huge sigh of relief washed over me. *"That's finally the end of this awful situation"* I thought.

No, no, no. Not only was she boasting all over social media about the new event business she had set up - which mimicked a lot of what ProspHER was doing (even using images of ProspHER's events to market this venture - the cheek!) - a week later I received an email from a solicitor. She's taking legal action against me! What the fuck! She tried to take money from a company that wasn't her money to take, then tried to keep a car that wasn't her car to keep - and she's blaming me?

It was no shock by then that I would be the person to blame for shit hitting the fan, even though I was nowhere near the fan to throw the shit in the first place! She was coming after me. But I was no longer playing the victim who could be easily manipulated and bullied.

At that time, I was more than halfway through my apprenticeship and I had learned so much. Not just the theoretical stuff about effective leadership and business growth strategies, but the practical stuff too - I trusted myself to make informed decisions, I believed in my own ability and intuition to solve problems, and most of all I had strengthened my mindset to be able to cope with mammoth challenges with ease.

I was no longer the frail wimp that could be talked around, pushed about, or blindsighted. I had grown a huge pair of balls and I was ready to swing them in whichever way I needed to.

So, I fought. I fought for myself. I fought for ProspHER. I fought for people everywhere who had lost their voice due to someone else making them feel small.

In September 2023, after countless emails, presentation of evidence and an employment tribunal, her claim for thousands upon thousands of pounds in compensation was reduced to a minimal amount, which - due to the closure of one division of ProspHER - was no longer applicable.

I had won. Not because she had lost her claim, but because I had learned so much from the whole process.

There are different sides to some people, which often are ugly in character and personality, but only surface when I'm not bending over backwards to please.

Because in this situation once I said *"no"* - and began to be true to myself and align with the long-term vision I had for my company - only then did "the Evil Queen" show her true colours.

Moving forwards, I would no longer trust anyone fully with the fate of my business. I would no longer give into every demand. I would never ignore my gut when making decisions.

I won because I finally understood my role to play in this complete facade, and I walked away wiser, stronger, braver and more resilient in my company than I had ever been before*(ish)*.

Emotional Wreck: Me completely hammered at a "Cowboys and Indians Themed Wine Club" night at my caravan site clubhouse, in mid-October 2022
(which was completely out of character for me, but drinking until I was sick through my nose was the only way I could deal with the incredible stress of the situation that had taken place over the months before).

Chapter 4 - My rock broke into pieces

As I just fast-forwarded a bit and skipped a huge chunk of late 2022 and early 2023, I want to pause and rewind again to keep this story flowing how it should.

On the same morning of the SUPERWOMAN Fest (before I escaped to the coast to hide from the world) I received a random email from someone I hadn't seen or worked with since many years before. The pandemic had meant we had lost touch and were not operating in the same circles as we used to.

Katie Oman had come back into my life the very same day that the aforementioned previous employee (aka "the Evil Queen") was due to exit it.

Pure coincidence, or the universe's way of aligning?

As you can imagine, from recent bad circumstances, I was feeling pretty alone at the time.

It was like I had been left holding the baby - and baby ProspHER was relentlessly crying. I knew I couldn't calm her down without some serious help!

And Katie was there at the right time to offer that.

With no hesitation, no judgement, no objections. Just pure support for no other purpose than to help (because she could see how desperately I needed it!)

Now, I'd like to say that during that time my faith in people had been restored and that I miraculously did a 360 and began to trust others again. But this wasn't the case. Along the whole of my business journey (that you will see from both my books), I have been stabbed in the back by people left, right and centre - usually because they get what they want from me then screw me over.

Maybe it's my fault for allowing them to do this to me again and again?

Anyway, I've noticed that every single time this has happened over the years, I've learnt something new about myself or my business from the negative situations. And this time was no different, as I had learned that trust had to be earned over a long period of time.

So, starting with Katie, I began to let more and more people into the business. But my boundaries were high, and my level of trust was low. I kept a close eye on everything that was going on. No matter how small the detail, I had a say in it.

I had turned over a completely new leaf. But, as a result, I'd become a complete control freak.

Christmas 2022 came and went (which was a difficult time due to the sudden passing of my beloved auntie Sonia after her short battle with cancer), so I welcomed the new year (and a clean slate) with my family on New Year's Eve - pre-celebrating my fresh-start and the opportunity to get my business and life on track with people that aligned with me and my values.

2023 started by planning the first ProspHER Fest event in Norwich, which built on the previous success of

ProspHER's events, but tweaked aspects and activities to become even better based on customer feedback.

In essence, this new-and-improved festival for female development was set to be SUPERWOMAN Fest on steroids!

Focusing on this distracted me from the grief I felt after losing my aunt, so in addition to helping the company thrive again after such troubling times, surrounding myself with great people and focusing on delivering positive impact was incredible therapy for me.

Planned for September 2023, this event was coming together nicely and we were well on our way to delivering its massive expectation.

Then, in mid-June, my family hit another huge bump in the road.

Bear in mind that I had been extremely ill during 2022, which had resulted in some severe bleeding from places I shouldn't have been bleeding (I don't want to give you too much information here) and a colonoscopy to check for cancer (which fortunately came back clear) - plus we were all in early stages of mourning our recent loss - I had felt like I had been trapped in a tidal wave that had shown no signs of slowing down. Over the last few years, it seemed that the waves had kept coming, over and over again, and I was being continuously dragged under, unable to gasp for air.

But, during early 2023, the seas had settled. Things were calm and on the up. I was relaxed.

To give you a tad bit of context, my husband Matthew (also known as my rock since I met him in 2011), had started to complain of severe headaches and a sore neck/shoulder a month or so earlier. Just putting it down to increased stress at work, the doctor advised him to take it easy and referred him to the physio for a check up.

Gradually, the headaches got worse; more intense. Matthew came home early from work and went straight to bed for a few nights in a row. This wasn't like him at all. He shortly became unable to sleep because of the increasing pain.

During one night, during the end of this difficult week, he woke me at 3am in the morning. He was shaking. He was clutching his head. He was in tears. A complete mess.

Now, I knew this situation was serious as I'd only ever seen Matthew cry once before at the funeral of a close family friend in all the years we had been together. Other than that, he had never shed a tear in his adult life.

The pain had taken control of him.

I immediately called the ambulance, who advised that they were extremely busy and, due to at least a 90 minute wait, it would be best to drive him to the hospital myself. The operator said that if anything changed with his symptoms then to call back. I hung up.

Ten minutes later, Matthew began to vomit dramatically. He was in and out of consciousness on the bathroom floor.

I dialled 999 again, and by 4am the ambulance arrived to take him to A&E at our local hospital.

My mum arrived to care for the kids so I could ride in the ambulance with Matthew.

He couldn't talk properly. His slurs didn't make any sense. The words *"potential stroke"* came from the paramedic's mouth. I tried to stay strong - holding back the tears behind my steamed-up glasses.

When we got to the hospital, Matthew had lots of tests and scans, which took all day into the evening. He had a fatal blood clot in his head, which had travelled from previous clots he'd had in his leg months and months earlier. He could have died. The love of my life, the father of my children, my best friend, my rock, could have left us forever.

It was a huge turning point in my life because, up until that point in time, I had taken this man for granted. I had always presumed he would be by my side. He had gotten me through some really hard times, and we had battled through the challenges of my previous divorce, losing babies, and the passing of loved ones, together - like a two-person army.

Amidst all of this, I had my final apprenticeship assessment day, twenty-four hours after Matthew first went into hospital, so I was studying when I could by his bedside and through the night so I could be ready for it. I'd worked so hard during the whole course leading up to this presentation and interview that I didn't want to fall at the last hurdle.

I tried to put Matthew to the back of my mind, and muddled through the online assessment as best I could. Coming off the online call, I just burst into tears.

What if my husband didn't make it through?

Visiting him in hospital a few days later with the children was a relief, as his pasty face I'd become used to had turned back to its usual perky colour, and he was more chatty and bright in personality. Copious amounts of strong painkillers and blood-thinners were his saviours, and he was soon back on the mend after a few weeks of rest.

A month later, I found out I'd earned a distinction grade for my level seven apprenticeship, which is an equivalent to a top-grade masters degree.

I did this, regardless of going through all the personal and professional issues I had faced.

With pure determination and relentlessness, I had overcome all the obstacles that I'd come up against, and my dedication to continuous learning (and pushing hard against my own boundaries) had paid off yet again.

I had powered through towards my goal and I had succeeded*(ish)*.

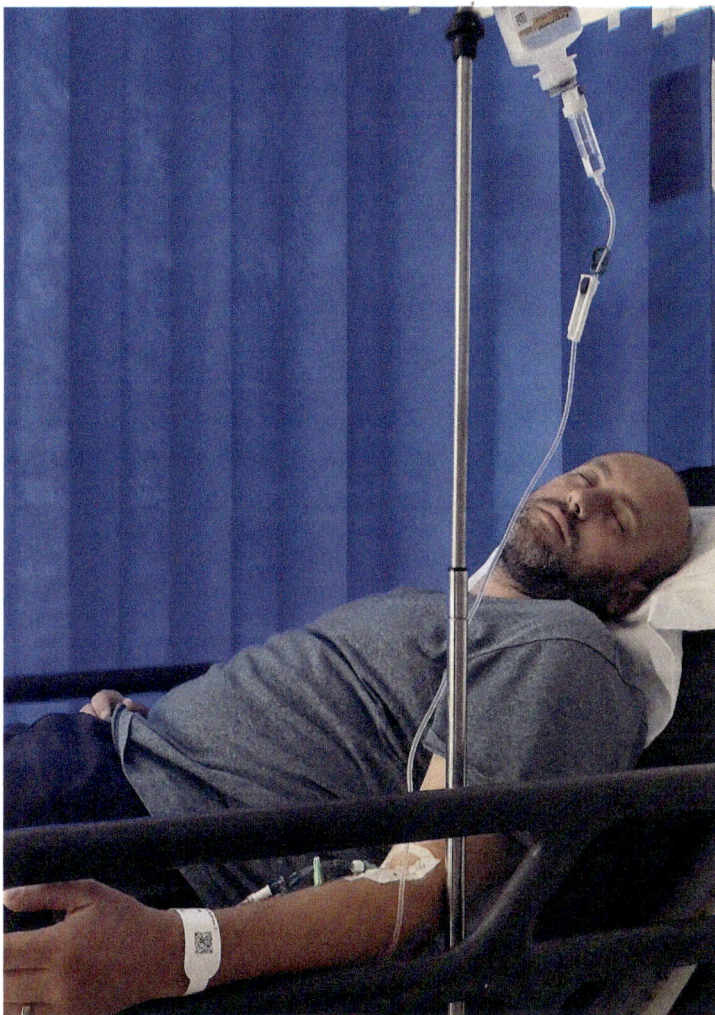

My Broken Rock: My husband Matthew on a painkiller drip
in hospital in June 2023, while I studied next to him, filled
with dread and worry.

Chapter 5 - Glueing the pieces back together

Back to business and, even though both my personal life and business world had fallen apart over the last year or so, I was optimistic that I could get things on track again.

By the latter part of 2023, ProspHER had hosted brilliant festival events in Ipswich, Colchester and Norwich, and with the support of Katie, then appointed as Event Director, we were recruiting other independent Event Managers to deliver these events in more locations across the UK.

I was speaking to so many different people about how we could develop and grow ProspHER, and being involved in Climb23 that summer had opened me up to new opportunities to network with those in the north of the country to widen our reach and expand.

It finally felt like the dark clouds of the past had lifted and conversations were becoming easier, due to the traction we had gained as an organisation, especially through the adversity we had faced.

Feedback from the calendar of events had led to the obvious conclusion that ProspHER's existing membership platform was no longer fit for purpose, and that it needed a huge revamp to reflect the innovation and evolution of the events side of our business.

So, I started reading and researching about raising equity investment, without realising that I was opening Pandora's box.

Up until that October, I had always bootstrapped my businesses, continuously investing my own earnings and working on side hustles and alternative roles to keep my business ventures growing. However, at that point, I decided that I didn't want to play it safe any longer. I wanted to go "all in".

Brainstorming and drawing up blueprint plans for the new-and-improved ProspHER Community platform, and beginning conversations about pulling together a business plan and pitch deck that was good enough to present to potential investors, I felt a mixture of emotions: excitement, confusion, fear. I realised quickly from speaking to numerous Venture Capital (VC) funds, angel groups and fundraising advisors that I was completely out of my depth.

Losing hope as I communicated with more and more "experts" in the fundraising circle, I vented my frustrations to a long-standing business contact of mine, Taylor Fordham (no relation to me, but a good friend and Brother from another Mother!)

Taylor asked me why I needed investment to make my ideas of an immersive and personalised learning platform for women's personal and professional development become a reality. *"Everything costs money"* was my response.

As a tech-genius who was more than capable of building such a platform, he wouldn't take no for an answer and agreed to create the structure and MVP (Minimum Viable Product) features to get things started.

I was beyond grateful.

The fact that someone believed in me enough to invest their time in creating what had only ever previously been a pipeline dream was incredible.

This opened my eyes to the fact that I didn't always have to be the one who was "the giver" in every professional relationship. For years I had jumped through hoops, people-pleased and given above and beyond in terms of time, money, kindness, knowledge and skills. It was finally my time to begin reaping the rewards from those I worked with, and start receiving in abundance for what I had put into the business.

Katie and Taylor had begun to reinforce my faith that there were good, trustworthy and reliable people in the world who just wanted to support me and ProspHER because they believed in the mission of *"educating and empowering one million women worldwide by 2030"*.

There didn't always have to be a selfish agenda*(ish)*.

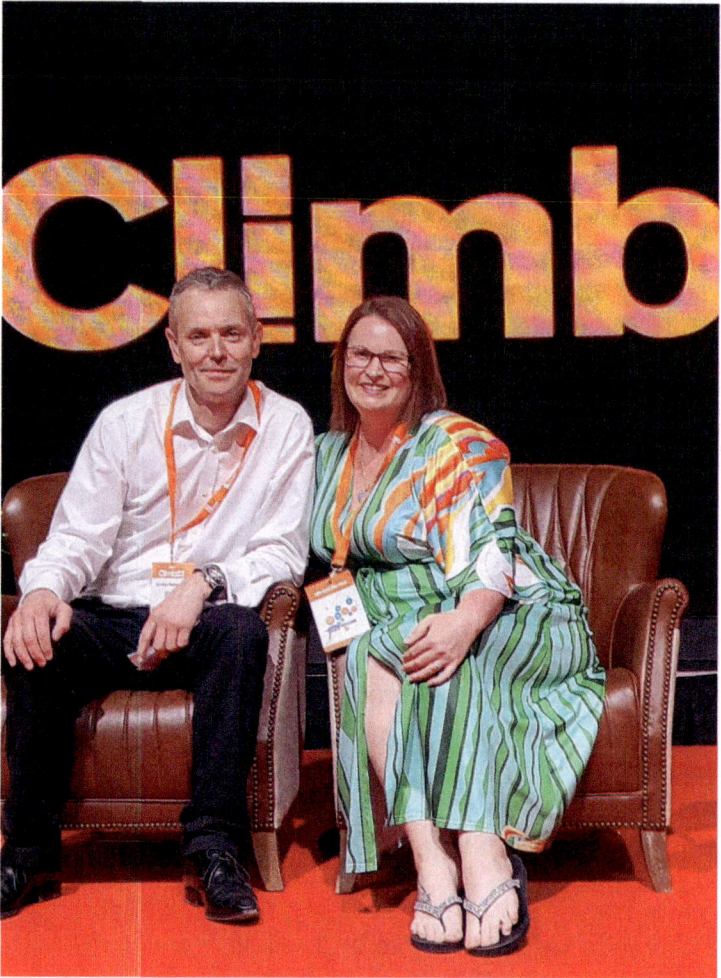

Taking The Stage: Me with Gordon Bateman (the organiser of Climb UK) at Climb23 in May 2023, where I hosted a panel discussion about DEI in the workplace.

Chapter 6 - Money, money, money

Even though Katie was a significant support on the in-person event-front, and Taylor had got the ball rolling in kick-starting the online community product build, there was still something missing. We were desperate for marketing and sales support - and for that, we still needed money.

We had a few volunteers undertaking social media management and seeking PR opportunities (thanks Katie Simms and Sarah Lloyd), but ProspHER's email marketing and CRM system was a complete mess and we had not sent an email to our sales leads for other a year (because this responsibility fell on me, and I had absolutely no idea about what I was doing!)

Due to this, I focused on finding someone to help with the email marketing, and continued the fundraising journey with an open mind.

I soon came across a woman via LinkedIn, who I'd been following for some time and felt she aligned well with ProspHER and our values, and we quickly got cracking on new email marketing, lead generation and social media campaigns to promote the new-and-improved ProspHER Community platform.

This was all well and good, but I desperately needed to find some money fast to keep the positive momentum of this going.

All the stats say that less than 2% of female-founders get funded, which is a pretty shit statistic and doesn't really motivate me into wanting to get out of bed every morning and into the inboxes of Angel Investors and Venture Capital firms.

I thought there was more gender equality, diversity and inclusion these days?

I think not when it comes to money!

Even so, I was focused on finding the right fit for me and ProspHER, so I did my research and went on a personal crusade to speak to as many people about equity funding as possible, in the hope that I would become less clueless about this topsy-turvy fundraising playground.

Now, I was used to the crazy highs and lows of scaling a business, however I really wasn't prepared for how many doors would get slammed in my face during my search for people to believe in my vision - and it proved even harder to convince those people who did share my values to back me by putting their hands in their pockets.

I fully appreciated that the pond of startup-founders seeking investment is bottomless, and that investors have to fish deep to find an opportunity which aligns with them - but I couldn't help wondering if there should have been a better way for business owners to find their right fit, other than the traditional outdated outreach and pitch process?

Spending hours, upon hours, away from my business - away from gaining new customers, away from building relationships with new partners, and away from developing the products and services that "brings home the bacon!" - all to create a pitch deck that required countless unnecessary revisions, navigating piles of legal paperwork covered in confusing jargon, and participating in pitch presentation rehearsals where each critique seemed to contradict the one before.

It all seemed like a complete waste of time, energy and focus to me - especially as I was going around-and-around in circles (like a puppy chasing its tail) and becoming increasingly frustrated with each "expert", consultant and investor I spoke to.

One day, I came across an article that shocked me, and heightened my frustration even further. It explained that the majority of founders that get funded end up closing their businesses within a few years anyway.

So, in reality, is the fundraising process a lot of effort for very little reward in the long run?

It definitely changed my perspective about how to bring more money into ProspHER, and at that point I pivoted to creating multiple income generation and fundraising streams (such as donations, social grants, Innovate UK funding, sponsorships, invoice financing, and Elite Founders Programme - where our members can invest into our community for financial return).

A brilliant book by Daniel H. Pink, *To Sell is Human*, really helped me to focus on making sales to increase business revenues, rather than prioritise external funding sources (so, I'd highly recommend giving this popular bestseller a read).

I decided that, even though I would continue to seek the right angel and VC investors for my business, I would no longer "put all my eggs in one basket" - which was an absolute killer move in diversifying and growing (if I do say so myself!)

As a side note, from my experience of "having it all" and "losing it all" in the past, I know the importance of building different pillars of income and diversifying investments to better accumulate wealth (i.e. from work, business, residential/commercial property, holiday letting, forex/stocks/shares trading, etc).

When it comes to your business, if you are currently seeking funding, I'd certainly recommend that you do the same and look at different ways to raise money that suits you and your business - rather than jumping on the equity fundraising bandwagon and investing too much time, energy and money into this as your soul mission (as I've seen way too many businesses - especially female-owned - run out of money and having to close because they lose perspective of what really matters).

On the flip-side, I've also come across many female-founders who have gained equity investment, but then had incredibly negative experiences, and some have lost everything they've worked for as a result.

Others who have also been successful in achieving funding rounds have said that (because they then had a large amount of cash in the bank) it made them wasteful, sloppy and frivolous - resulting in reduced growth than expected (especially in comparison to if they had continued to bootstrap and expanded steadily).

I'd also like to add that there also seems to be quite a "throw-away mindset" related to equity investment. For example, one advisor told me that many startups tend to raise money to build an MVP product for marketplace testing purposes, then completely scrap it and build a completely new-and-improved product.

Again, this seems such a massive waste of time, energy and money, when investment could be allocated to more established organisations (like ProspHER - hint, hint!), who have already tested and refined their products and services within the marketplace over time - using their own money, time, and resources (thus backing themselves 100% to prove what can be achieved without investment).

Now, I want to pause here and call myself out for being such a "negative-nelly" about all things equity investment up until this point. Mainly because it isn't all bad, and however you fund your business, it still needs money coming from somewhere, right?!

Plus, some people and resources have really helped me through this journey - shout out to James Church (who has written a great book called *Investable Entrepreneur* that he gives away for free via Robot Mascot's website), Sam Simpson from Founder Catalyst (who provides some great free resources on their website too), and the EHE Group and associates (who have compiled a super informative book named *Fast Growth Through Funding*).

Innovate UK Edge and Grantify are also helpful when looking into Innovate UK funding, and there are also some great bid-writing and financing companies, support groups, and fundraising directories out there (I like using Swoop) to find alternative sources of finance that align with your mission and values. Feel free to contact me through the ProspHER website if you'd like any more advice or recommendations!

Anyway, getting back on track - you will notice from my short eight month experience with fundraising (which pretty much is the same with most things in business) that the opinions of other people, companies, etc, are just that - opinions.

The perspective of one person won't be the same as the view of another and, once I realised this and stopped following every single piece of advice I'd received, the more focused and confident I became. It was only when I began to trust my own judgement and intuition to make business decisions (including those about what funding avenues suited best), I felt more clarity about the future direction of ProspHER than ever before.

So, what I'm getting at is that, although it is good to gain knowledge and guidance from lots of sources, it can often end up being counterproductive (and a complete time-sucker!) - therefore, be methodical and selective through this process. Above all, trust your own judgement because, ultimately, you are the one who knows your business (and work) better than anyone.

In a nutshell, I recommend defining what priorities you have for your business, career and life, rather than looking at others to tell you what success looks like to you. It's all about the trade-off between time and money, and what you see as important.

In hindsight, I wish I had confirmed to myself that my time is much more valuable to me before starting my fundraising journey in November 2023, because I feel I would have done a lot of things differently, so that my time investment didn't have as much impact on my wellbeing and lifestyle, especially taking the time away from spending with my family and friends, and doing the things I really enjoy (like dog-walking on the beach/in the woods, meals with friends, and spa days with my mum).

Plus, establishing my priorities and boundaries beforehand would have allowed me to be super selective on what truly aligned with myself and my vision of ProspHER, thus maximising the experience to its full potential.

But, "c'est la vie", hey!

I value what I've learned from the whole process, and I continue to learn to enable me to share my insights to help others (including you).

Right now, I'm much more at peace and relaxed, because I'm fully prioritising the things in my life and business that really matter to me, and know that the right opportunities to attract income into my company are steadily presenting themself to me - which becomes even more important as I continue to share my story with you in the next chapter.

Well, sort of *(ish)*.

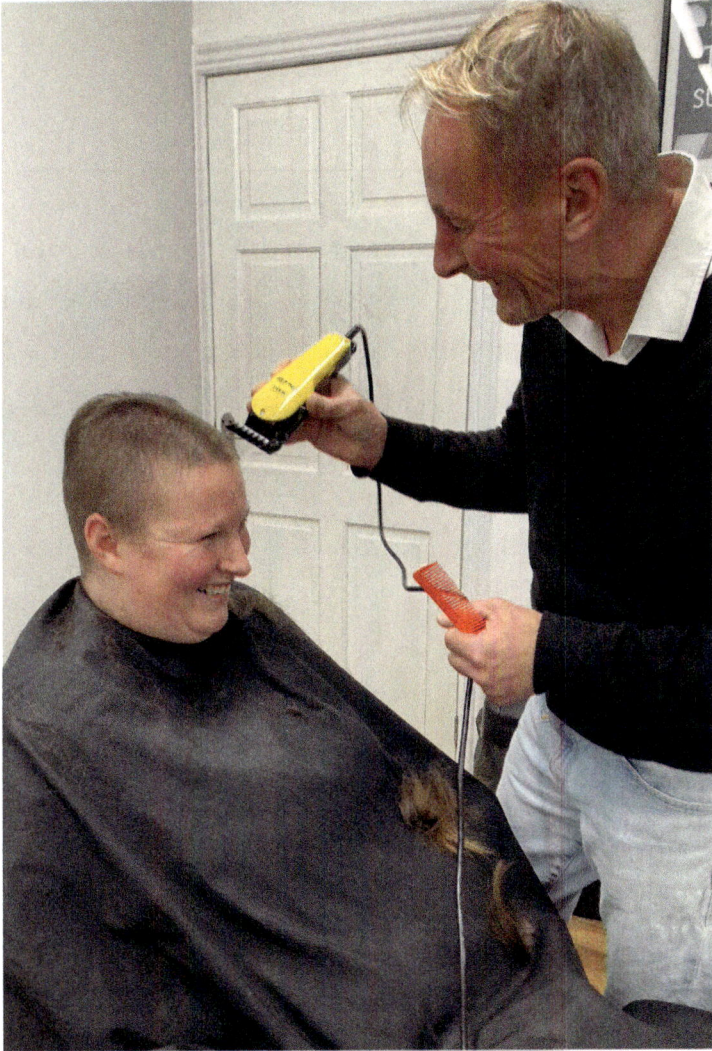

Braving The Shave: My dad shaving my head in memory of my auntie Sonia, in December 2023.

Chapter 7 - Crashing down all around

I'd marked 2024 as the year that I would fulfil more of my aspirations than ever before.

I'd decided that I'd put other people first for so long and, because I'd never made myself a priority, this had resulted in the majority of challenges I had faced over the past few years.

I was putting myself in my own way. And my dreams will never be accomplished if I continued to do things the same way.

But, as the clock struck midnight on 31st December, I felt liberated with my newly shaved head from "Braving the Shave" in memory of my auntie Sonia a few weeks before, and highly optimistic that this year was going to be "my year".

Based on my past experience of juggling female entrepreneurship, motherhood, and my various other roles as a woman, I wasn't under any illusions that even though I'd decided to focus more on myself and what I wanted in my life this year, there would still be some ups and downs.

Little did I know that I needed to buckle up and strap myself in more tightly than ever - as 2024 was going to be my bumpiest ride yet!

In the November before, I had landed on my lower back during a "clip-and-climb" session with my children. Feeling absolutely fine, and not giving it another thought over the festive season, I didn't put two and two together when I started getting shooting pains across my back and down my right leg early in January.

I distinctly remember the day of the 16th January 2024 being one of my lowest yet. My manic depression had reared its ugly head on various occasions over the years - especially after birthing both of my two children, each of the separate times I lost my three babies, and at various intervals where I'd faced negative work situations and trouble in relationships.

But this particular day was darker than I'd witnessed in a while.

I had cried on and off for most of the day and, after my family had all gone to sleep, I was left laying in the same spot that I'd occupied on the sofa for the past few weeks.

My body had even made a divot in the sofa cushions, and unable to move (other than to drag my painful leg behind me to the bathroom) I had become confined to this grey fabric prison. I ate there, slept there, spent every single day there - feeling overwhelming pain stabbing me in the lower back and pulsing down my leg, like electricity shocking every cell.

The more I laid there, the more time I had to think. Thinking about the chronic pain. Thinking about how useless I had become. Thinking about how everyone around me was carrying on with their lives and mine was just frozen in time.

And the more I thought, the deeper into my own black hole I fell.

At 11:56pm on 16th January I wondered how much paracetamol I would need to take to stop all the thinking and put an end to it all.

But, of course I didn't go through with my end of life fantasy.

I had children that were reliant on me, a home that I'd created, and a business that I'd built - I wasn't about to give up on everything and let this situation win.

The sciatica had reached a new level of intensity by mid-February and, after a trip to my local A&E, I was booked in for an MRI scan to check what was going on with my back.

In an appointment with my doctor a week after, he confirmed that I had herniated discs that were agitating my sciatic nerve and that I would need some physiotherapy to help relieve the issue.

But, I didn't make it to my first physio appointment.

The pain had reached unbearable levels. I couldn't sleep. I couldn't eat. I had headaches that turned into migraines. I was being sick. My body had gone into complete shock.

Over the third weekend in February, I lost all feeling in my right leg.

Sciatica pain had begun electrocuting my left leg, and the pins and needles attacking my left foot were intense.

I wet myself multiple times over that weekend.

Yes, a thirty-five year old woman wetting herself like a two year old.

I had officially reached a state of rock bottom.

After that weekend, on the Monday evening, Matthew came home from work to find me stuck on the sofa, unable to move, stripped of my mobility. So, off to the hospital we went again.

A&E was busy as usual, and the longer we sat in the waiting room, the more pain I felt in my back and the less sensation I felt in my legs.

Finally, through to see the doctors, I had lots of different tests, and was asked again and again to explain what had happened.

Bored of telling the same story to everyone I met, I was relieved when I was finally sent through to the musculoskeletal unit, who did some movement tests before sending me to a ward just after 12:00am.

Matthew had gone home by that point, and I was so starving after not eating all day that I engulfed a below-standard plain cheese sandwich as a midnight snack, washed down with a side of heavy painkillers to take the edge off the pain.

I actually slept well until the breakfast hustle and bustle woke me in the morning.

I wasn't allowed to order breakfast as I was to have nil by mouth until after my MRI scan that had been booked in for 7:30am to investigate what was causing my intense pain and loss of sensation from the waist down.

The smell of food was making my stomach rumble (especially because the cheese between two dry pieces of bread didn't quite satisfy me during the night), but the pain soon distracted me from my hunger.

Even though I had so many other patients, doctors, nurses, and other staff buzzing around me, I felt completely alone. Confused. Isolated. Exhausted.

The scan was pretty quick and straightforward, and I was soon back on the ward within an hour of being taken down by the porter.

Calmness had resumed after the breakfast rush, and everyone seemed much more relaxed than before I'd left, with the only sounds around my bed coming from the beeping of machines and soft chatter of nurses.

Before I knew it, chaos flooded my bay.

People came from every direction.

They swiftly pulled across my curtains, covered my body in loads of sticky patches, and hooked me up to an ECG machine to monitor my heart rate.

I didn't know what was going on.

I glanced at the clock and it was 8:42am.

Two doctors started talking at me, saying that my scan had shown that one of my spinal disks had severely herniated and was pressing on my sciatic nerve (a condition known as "Cauda Equina Syndrome").

The pressure of the disk in my lower back was cutting off the feeling in my lower body.

Shoving a form in my face and asking me to sign it, I tried to focus and read what it said.

But, my attention was occupied by the words that were spoken by the doctor next.

"If we operate on your spine then there is a risk that you could become permanently paralysed, but if we

don't then you will definitely lose all functions of your lower body."

Without much of a choice, I signed the waiver without hesitation.

Glancing at the clock to my left again, over the shoulders of the staff unhooking me from the ECG machine, I saw it was then 8:51am.

Before the pen ink had dried, my bed sidebars were pulled up and I was in transit to the operating theatre.

The last five minutes had spun my head into a whirlwind.

One minute I was relaxing while being pumped full of more painkillers, and the next I was being whisked through corridors, in and out of lifts, and through swinging double doors to meet my surgeons.

There was no time to dwell. No time to think. No time to tell my loved ones what was going on.

As the head surgeon explained the operation to me, fear flashed through my mind.

What if I never woke up?

I hadn't even had the chance to say goodbye to Matthew, my kids, or my parents, let alone the rest of my family and friends.

What if I never got the chance to see them all again?

I sobbed as I was put to sleep.

When I opened my eyes, they locked with a pair of bright blue eyes of a friendly nurse smiling back at me.

She touched my arm to comfort me as I gradually came round to focus on the recovery room surroundings.

Feeling relaxed but in a false sense of control, I tried to lift up my head to get a better view of this new environment, but my head felt heavy, leaving me dizzy and woozy.

Not wanting to vomit everywhere, I settled my head back down while the nurse explained the outcome of my procedure. However, I couldn't concentrate on her words at all because my brain was fully preoccupied in instructing my toes to perform a gentle wiggle.

The realisation that I wasn't paralysed changed my perspective of life completely in that moment*(ish)*.

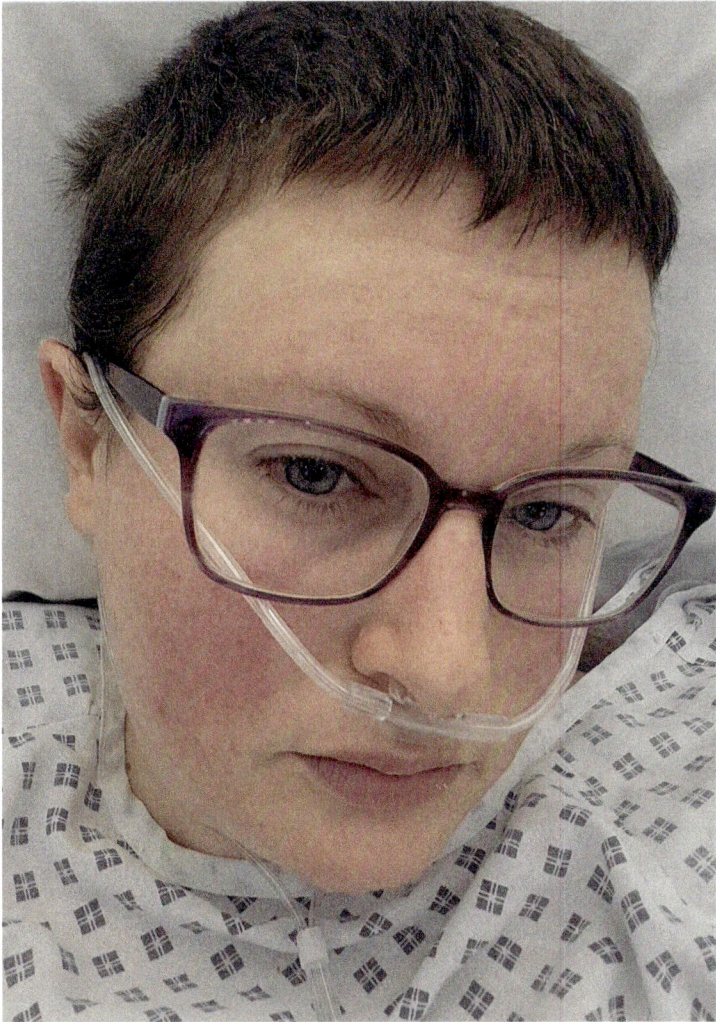

Uncomfortably Numb: Me waking up very disoriented after my emergency surgery at the end of February 2024.

Chapter 8 - Kick me while I'm wounded

I was grinning from ear to ear as I was wheeled into another ward.

Still moving my toes and flexing my angles, which had been an unfamiliar sensation only a few hours before, I was reversed into the left-hand middle bay and reconnected to oxygen and hooked up to other monitors for observation.

My feet were aching and throbbing. Exhausted from their extensive workout.

I was relieved to be alive.

I thanked God for saving me.

I prayed for strength in my recovery.

The surgeon visited my bedside to tell me the discectomy and decompression surgery had been a success and, after some physiotherapy, I should be able to go home within two weeks.

Visits from Matthew, my kids, my parents and my cousin, support from the healthcare team, friendliness from my neighbouring patients, and my own sheer will and determination, kept me going through the long days and even longer nights.

After getting on my feet that same evening, sitting upright and standing the next day, and walking the day after that (much before the physios anticipated I would do), I made it out of hospital after just four days.

Driving home felt like every bump in the road was causing an invisible screwdriver to jab into my lower back, but all I could do was smile. I was surrounded by my family and I could (admittedly very stumbly), stand and walk.

Back at home, I soon settled into a completely new routine to accommodate my medical situation, and with intense help and assistance from Matthew, my kids, my parents and my in-laws, I gradually began to toilet, wash and dress myself.

Within the next month, and still on many painkillers a day, I managed to navigate around using the furniture (much like a toddler learning to walk).

I was popping paracetamol like they were sweeties, as I was unable to take anything stronger because opioids made me violently sick. I slept for most of each day, while tossing and turning in pain and discomfort each night. However, I was so grateful for my increasing independence.

While I was in this early rehabilitation stage, ProspHER hadn't completely gone to pot. Katie and Taylor were very much still involved - keeping both the events side of the business and the online learning community afloat - but marketing had fallen flat because this was a responsibility that fell on my shoulders.

It became very apparent that I needed to offload this burden completely while I recovered, therefore the email marketing freelancer we had been working with since November seemed like a good fit (let's call her "B" - I've kept her name a secret because I don't kiss and tell!)

Even though I didn't know of her personally, she came recommended through my network as the "go-to" woman for marketing. As she seemed to align with the company's values and understood our mission, she set to work on our marketing strategy to take this mammoth task off my incapable hands.

To be able to afford this extra support, the business took out a loan, but with the promise of targeted results, sent to me in writing by "B", I was confident that the ROI (return on investment) would soon cover the monthly repayments (and some!)

"B" had signed ProspHER up to an expensive CRM (Customer Relationship Management) system, as apparently our existing one was not reliable at reporting and delivering trustworthy data that could be property analysed.

Despite this new software costing more than ten times of our previous one, I trusted the "expert" and continued to believe her that the sales would soon be flooding in and the results would dramatically outweigh the high costs.

By April 2024, the business bank account was drier than "Gandhi's flip-flop", and with minimal sales resulting from "B's" efforts, there was very little income coming in to cover the crippling costs.

In addition, because I wasn't working due to my rehab, I didn't have any money to lend to the company (which is what I had historically done in times like this before).

I raised my concerns to "B" on several occasions due to the lack of results the email marketing was generating compared to the KPIs (Key Performance Indicators) she had sent to me months before.

I scraped funds together from dribs and drabs to try to keep things afloat, but this was having a detrimental affect on my already fragile mental health.

After countless messages, emails and long phone calls with "B" throughout April, and continued promises that *"results will just take a little longer"*, I decided it was best for us to part ways - so I was left holding the "debt baby" like I had done a few times on my business journey before.

In hindsight, and if I had been thinking clearer during this turbulent time in my life, I would have never took out the loan, agreed to switch to a new CRM system (of which I didn't realise the contract tie in) or trusted someone in this way again (after my experience with "the Evil Queen" that I told you about earlier).

I was disappointed that I didn't listen to my gut.

I had believed the promises (and lies) of another person that didn't have my best interests at heart, and took advantage of my situation.

One evening at the end of April, just after my 36th birthday, I had a complete pity-party on my "sofa prison".

I replayed what had happened with "B" over and over in my head, I regretted my naive decisions, and I seriously considered whether the business that I've spent so many years building was really my destiny.

I sat there alone, red in the face, tears streaming from my eyes, questioning it all.

Was everything in my life what I actually wanted?

Did all I'd worked for even excite me anymore?

Was running a business worth all the difficult days?

Could I actually make the money I desired to materialise all the great things I had on my vision board?

After a few hours of crying into a pillow (so I didn't wake my family), I came to the conclusion that this wasn't my first rodeo!

I'd had a few times like this since I founded my first company in 2013.

In fact, at least three times yearly, in eleven years.

So, I decided I would do what I did all those times before, and pick myself up, dust myself off, and make a plan to confidently move forwards.

The next day, out of nowhere, randomly a woman who I wasn't hugely familiar with, Sandra Anderson, raised her hand in the Event Team Whatsapp Group to volunteer to help me with the marketing, in the attempt to salvage the mediocre work from the last few months (which turns out had mostly been completed by a Virtual Assistant, rather than "B" herself).

Sandra had only been an Event Manager at ProspHER for a few months, but I'd heard she was already making valuable contributions to the team and sharing ideas that were improving processes and operations.

And, by piping up and sharing with me that she had previously been involved in improving user experience (UX) for EE, this showed she had experience that was just as impressive as her humbleness.

Now, I don't want to paint Sandra as an angel sent from Heaven to fix our marketing problems (as she will tell you herself that she is slightly naughty and mischievous), but I admit that she came at just the point where I was ready to give up and throw in the "business-towel" altogether - so I'm eternally grateful.

ProspHER had been created from a long journey of negatives, strung together by the occasional "win", but I knew that even though I was at a low point - physically, mentally and emotionally - giving up was still not on the agenda!

At that pivotal moment, this reinforced how influential it was to have people really rooting for me.

I took a metaphorical look around me, and rather than focusing on what and who I had lost, I honed in on all those who really believed in me (even during the "slumps" when I didn't believe in myself).

This was truly one of the most powerful messages I could have received at that time.

When I felt at the lowest of the low, the belief and support of Sandra (and the rest of "Team ProspHER") got me through, and changed the entire trajectory of the business - and the rest of my life.

My failures were not rejection at all, but actually redirection towards new opportunities.

This reinforced my resilience, and gave me a new lease of strength and hope when I needed it the most.

And my emerging faith confirmed to me that everything would just naturally work out*(ish)*.

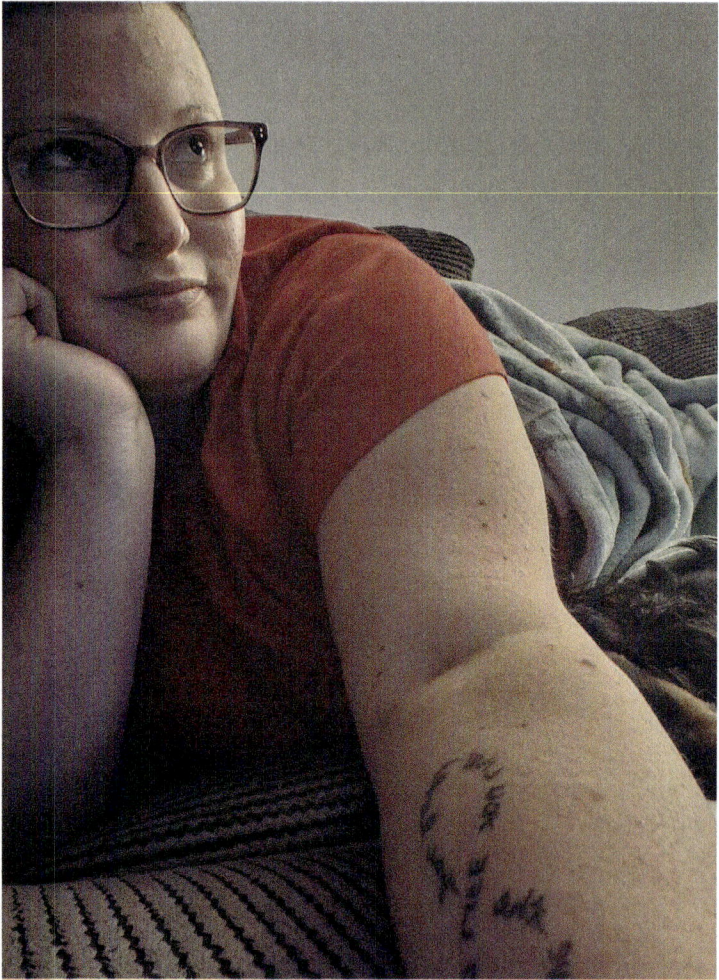

My "Sofa Prison": Me laid up in the lounge during my recovery in early-March 2024, feeling useless, depressed and in a great deal of pain.

Chapter 9 - Burn the MF'in house down!

Even in the brittle state I was in, I had been able to steer the business ship back into calmer waters.

However, in my personal life it had not only rained, but completely pissed it down.

And the "rain" continued to pour until I was drowning.

In late 2023, my brother had gone through some "relationship stuff" that continued into the new year, my mum was awaiting heart bypass surgery since the previous year, and early in 2024 we'd found out that Matthew's auntie, grandma and grandad all had been diagnosed with different types of cancer.

It was an extremely worrying time for myself, Matthew, and both of our immediate families.

And, on top of the impacts of my surgery, this sent our emotions into boiling point.

The stress was unmanageable.

2024 continued to flood us with misfortune.

On a dark evening the day after Matthew's birthday in March, myself, Matthew and the children were relaxing in front of the TV. The clock had just struck 9pm, and based on the amount of yawning our bedtime was imminent.

As per my request, my son walked over to the kitchen bin to dispose of his sweet wrappers. In the next second he shouted louder than I'd ever heard him shout before.

"Fire!!!"

We instantly all sprung into action. Jumping up off the sofa, Matthew ran to open our back door to meet a face full of red, yellow and orange.

Flames had already engulfed our neighbour's garage and were making their way across our garage roof.

I called 999 to be told that the fire brigade were only minutes away, then swiftly moved the kids and the dog into my bedroom at the front of our bungalow to keep as far away from the devastation as possible.

Matthew ran across the road to find our elderly neighbour, who was visiting his recently-blinded brother that evening, and banged on the window to highlight the emergency going on opposite.

Due to my incapacity and intense pain, I was stuck laying on my bed, while trying to calm Buddy the dog, who was in an agitated state. My children watched from the window and communicated what was happening outside, as two fire engines arrived into our cul-de-sac and people in fire uniforms jumped out and raced with their water hoses towards the epicentre of the chaos.

After two and a half hours of drenching the raging flames, the fire was finally out.

Our neighbour had admitted to the fire crew during the kerfuffle that he'd put hot ashes in his wheelie bin that sat between our garages that afternoon, thinking they had cooled enough to dispose of, hence accidentally setting them alight.

The next morning, in agony from moving too quickly the evening before, I hesitantly opened my back door and looked out to witness the aftermath of the unsettled night. What was left stood the charred remnants of our neighbour's garage structure, and the burnt roof of our garage hanging off in shame.

The smell of smoke consumed my lungs with every inhalation.

I closed the door and burst into tears, overwhelmed by yet another shitty thing that had blown up in my life.

Even though dealing with the house insurance claim was a complete pain in the arse (these things are never easy right?!), upon reflection I felt blessed that no one was hurt (or worse) from the incident.

A few weeks of more bed rest passed, and without much time at all to process recent events, negativity raised its ugly head yet again.

Later in March, my mum's long-awaited heart bypass surgery was finally scheduled.

It was planned to take place at a specialist heart unit in Cambridge, which was over an hour from me, and, as my surgery had left me unable to travel, I couldn't go with her for the procedure or week-long stay.

Early on the morning of her operation, my mum called me to say that all was going according to plan, and that my dad had just left her in the waiting room, where she was killing time reading until she went down to theatre.

Throughout that day, I had more conversations with my dad than I'd had with him over the past year. He wasn't usually a "talker" over the phone, so I guessed he needed my pointless babble to distract him from his intense worry.

Expecting to hear something by late afternoon, me and my brother were beginning to panic - texting each other every five minutes to attempt to console one another, and make excuses to justify the longer than expected wait.

Time was ticking by so slowly.

It was well into the evening, and we still hadn't heard anything from the hospital. My dad was becoming a nervous wreck, and me and my brother were running out of believable explanations as to why the hospital still hadn't been in touch.

Mum had been in theatre for over seven hours.

The 26th of March 2024 was officially becoming the longest day of my life.

Waiting for my dad to call me to say those hopeful three words - *"everything is alright"* - was excruciating.

If my legs had allowed me to pace the floor, I would have done.

I probably would've worn a hole in the rug too!

I held my breath for what seemed like forever when my phone rang and the words *"Dad Mob"* flashed across the screen.

She was OK. Surgery was a success. Crisis over. Phew.

Tragedy had passed and seven days later mum was home to begin her recovery.

Unfortunately, it wasn't the last time that my family would see the inside of a hospital in 2024, as it seemed that Matthew's grandma wasn't responding well to her treatment, and by Easter she was rapidly going downhill in hospital.

Over the bank holiday weekend, myself and Matthew visited her by her bedside, along with his parents, brother, auntie and grandad (who were still both frequently visiting the outpatients department to receive their own cancer treatments).

Entering her private room nearly shocked my "plastered on" fake smile cleanly off my face. It broke my heart to see how thin and frail she had become since I'd seen her only a few months earlier.

I held back the tears while making small talk and glancing awkwardly between Matthew and each of his family members. It felt like we were in a zoo, gorping at a helpless animal suffering in their enclosure.

We could do nothing but watch.

Even so, this sombre encounter around grandma's "death-bed" engraved a beautiful memory in my mind for eternity - Matthew's grandad softly clutching his wife's hand to comfort her through the immense fear and uncertainty.

In that moment, my sole aspiration was to have a loving relationship with Matthew that was as stable and strong as theirs was, well into our elderly stages of life.

I never saw grandma again after that visit. She peacefully (on her birthday) lost her short battle with the dreadful illness a week later.

The funeral was a stunning testament to her life and the valuable work she had done with the Women's Institute.

And, witnessing Matthew's grandad pausing to lovingly place his hand on the end of her coffin, for one final time before he exited the chapel, instantly took me back to the heartfelt moment between them I'd cherished from the hospital visit.

Welcoming the warm sun of May was a timely distraction from recent dark events and, in the attempt to move forwards positively, I dug deep to find the strength I needed to rise again*(ish)*.

Up In Smoke: When my neighbour accidentally set our garages alight in mid-March 2024, while I was still stuck in my house after my surgery
(Matthew didn't show me this photo until the fire was out, as he didn't want to panic me, so I was oblivious to how ferocious the flames were).

Chapter 10 - Seeing the wood from the trees

I'd faced so much crap in such a short space of time that my delicate mental state had become a continuous battle.

My brain mimicked a yo-yo, with my emotions fluctuating up-and-down - day-by-day, hour-by-hour, and even sometimes minute-by-minute.

I phased in and out of the same black hole that had presented itself during several occasions of torment over the last few years.

As Summer loomed, dragging myself away from the eclipsing darkness (and determined to put the terrible year thus far behind me), I decided that stalling in life was no longer a viable option.

I was hesitant to move on (and hopefully upwards) from the chaos, carefully considering whether jumping in with both feet, like I'd done so many times before, would cause me to sink or swim.

But, surely if I didn't push forwards with my dreams then how would I ever know?

So, I pulled up my "big girl pants" and came to the conclusion that negative thoughts would no longer drag me down.

Using the last couple of months as my motivation, I began to focus on all the positive learnings that I'd gained from the recent health-related dramas and losing a dear loved one.

I also recalled all the amazing things that had happened in my life, highlighted all the challenges I'd overcome, and celebrated all the accomplishments I'd achieved so far.

Journalling the thoughts and feelings as I remembered them, truly put my life in perspective, and reminded me that there were so many more important things that took priority over work, business, money and "superficial shit".

All the "bull-plop" meant absolutely nothing when I started to really see and understand the bigger picture.

I was sure that the universe had sent me all of the misfortune to teach me some valuable lessons, while presenting me with gifts (such as Sandra) at the exact times I needed them to remind me not to give up on my dream life.

As well as taking hold of the marketing reins for the business, at this pivotal time, Sandra, as a talented tarot reader (and also Katie for that matter), also reminded me how powerful spiritualism could be for healing my mind and body.

Now, as a side note, I used to be very sceptical of any "woo-woo" type stuff (journalling included), and would have called myself a "realist" a few years before. However, I had dabbled in the world of spiritualism a tad before - practising meditation, visualisation, affirmations and gratitude - and wasn't closed off to getting back on that "horse" again.

Since processing my internal dialog on a daily basis in writing was starting to make me feel lighter and freer, I started meditating again. Using visualisation to get in touch with my deeper intuition, and calling on the law of attraction to improve the company's financial drama.

By the way, if you are new to this "spiritual stuff" and want to explore it to see if it aligns with you (p.s. I know what it's like to be sceptical, but these things are worth a shot right!) then two of my favourite people to listen to are Mary Kate - for affirmations and subliminals - and Esther Hicks - for manifestations - (just search for them both on YouTube!)

Well, what can I say? Gradually incredible things started to happen.

Making decisions about the future was becoming easier and easier, and I had a sense of regained control that I hadn't felt in a long while.

I'd actually go as far as saying that "magical" things started to happen!

Throughout June, money started arriving from unexpected places. Random sales happened out of thin air.

Dreamlike prayers I'd had for years (such as my daughter being able to see Taylor Swift on tour) became reality.

Things were unreal. Huge. Extraordinary.

All materialising before my eyes.

And, I had no other way of explaining them than the work I was doing on myself in terms of connecting to my spiritual-self (and my Romany Gypsy heritage).

But, remember that I'd learnt that money and material stuff was far from the "be-all-and-end-all"?

Well, because I was wise to that fact, I knew I had to be careful that any financial abundance coming my way didn't get in the way of my number one priorities (aka my health and family).

Yes, I admit that money does tend to make living easier, offers more choices, and means sleeping better (free of those dreaded money worries), but it doesn't necessarily equal happiness - especially not when it came to my happiness. Some special care, consideration and preparation needed to be taken.

So, as a loyal cheerleader of continuous learning, and while I had a little spare time on my hands (whilst still in recovery), I set my sights on brushing up on my financial "know-how" and seeking new ways to better position ProspHER for its sustainable future.

Reading some useful books, namely *Profit First*, *SYSTEMology* and *From the Factory Floor*, helped me to understand money and processes better - and beginning to embed these ideologies into my reality only strengthened the incredible outcomes that were surfacing from tapping into my subconscious mind (with all the inner "woo-woo" work I was doing).

This provided me with proof of something I'd suspected for many years - that balancing practical systems with spiritual elements (and both "divine masculine" traits and "divine feminine" characteristics - just search for this online if you don't understand what I mean here!) can work in total harmony together, and there is a place for both to coincide to achieve my aspirations faster than ever.

With this newfound perspective, I felt more powerful than ever before.

I'd reached the ultimate epiphany that all the things that had happened (the "good, bad and the ugly") in my life to get me to July 2024 were all meant to be.

To get me to this exact point of enlightenment*(ish)*.

Acknowledging My Accomplishments: Me at the Broadland and South Norfolk Business Awards in March 2023 after ProspHER had won the "Collaboration Award".

Chapter 11 - Embracing my warts and all

We've now reached present day in my story - August 2024 - the brightest and most stunning month of the year (well, for me living in the UK, anyway!)

And hasn't it been a bumpy ride?

But, I made it. I got here. And, I lived to tell the tale.

My new realisation that all the things I'd recently wished for have magically become real, and understanding that any plot twist was just directing me around a hazard and towards something even better, is a breath of fresh air.

I am now exhaling a big sigh of relief.

Especially as writing this book has brought up some intensely awful memories all over again.

It's been an exhausting journey.

One that isn't quite over yet, but I know I'm well on my way.

As they say - you get what you focus on - so keeping my eyes on the good stuff going on, and getting through the bad stuff as best I can, is my mantra moving into late 2024 and beyond.

My next focus is improving my health, which you know has suffered dramatically lately - but using body scanning (mixed with traditional physiotherapy), I am slowly healing, and regaining strength in my back and legs day-by-day (although I'm ready for a long road ahead).

Now is the time where I put my selflessness aside, and write *"me"* at the very top of my priority list.

I will always put my oxygen mask on before helping others with theirs (metaphorically speaking), as I know far too well the detrimental costs to my health and wellbeing for trying to fill other peoples' cups (again metaphorically speaking) when mine is completely empty.

(Quick shameless plug: I talk a lot about this in my first book, HER Funny Business, so give it a look if you've not read it yet!)

Speaking of putting *"me"* at the top of my priority list - I'd like to state something here for the record.

I'm me, and I'm damn proud of it.

There, I said it.

That's something I never thought I'd hear coming out of my mouth.

Growing up, little Serena was shy, didn't have many friends and was bullied into adulthood.

I always had more self-doubt and hatred for myself than I could shake a stick at (why do they say this phrase? It's weird, but I like it!)

And, this doubt has led to severe imposter syndrome throughout my experiences of being a business leader.

I have often found myself in rooms or circumstances where I told myself I wasn't "good enough".

So, as you can suspect, from this core belief, and with the crazy stuff that I've battled through over the last few years, the last thing I would have thought I'd have learned was to like myself.

Regardless of all the shit that life had thrown at me, I realised that above everything, I really do truly, wholeheartedly, completely and unapologetically love myself.

Warts and all.

In fact, I'd even go as far as saying that I think I'm pretty - no absolutely - fabulous!

Not in an arrogant or cocky way, but in a way that I finally accept myself as the person that I am. Inside and out.

Staying real, authentic, humble and true to myself.

No matter what life throws in my way.

And I pledge to continue to be kind, supportive, nurturing, impactful - and always cheer on others to succeed.

My love for knowledge, my fun-loving nature, and my creative and innovative edge will keep me moving forwards.

Even through the tough times.

And, by embracing the views, opinions and challenges from others - always listening and learning (plus, not being completely up my own arse!) - I know I will find my way.

However uneven my path gets.

I also now view my weaknesses as my strengths - my new superpowers.

When my depression rears its ugly head, this no longer sends me into a spiral of self-sabotage, but instead provides a catalyst for me to take time out to reflect and prioritise, before moving into "action mode" again.

Most importantly, I have come to appreciate the importance of letting go. Letting go of people, stuff and situations that no longer serve me. Those that no longer add value to my life, or make me a better person in any way.

I now simply prevent what isn't a "good fit" for me from being part of my journey - keeping my barriers high (and my chin up) - while leaving behind anything or anyone that no longer aligns with who I am, and who I'm becoming.

Examples of this recently are, rejecting new clients and projects, leaving my sideline career as a College Business Lecturer (a dream I'd had since I was in high school, but turns out that "teaching in traditional educational settings" isn't really for me) , and saying farewell to two of my "closest friends" (who turned out not to be so "close") over the past year - one because she didn't contact me at all when I needed her during my turbulent time in early 2024, and one because her actions and behaviour didn't align at all with my morals and values.

Realising that "losing" these things from my life wasn't losing at all, because, by respecting myself first, I was actually winning every time.

As a bit of advice, if you haven't evaluated what and who are on your journey - and why - lately, then I strongly suggest giving this reflective exercise a go, as letting go of what doesn't serve you will really help you to develop and grow as a person (on so many levels).

Plus, with all the spare space in your life after your "little clear out", you can spend more time with the people that uplift you, and doing the things that make you truly happy.

This activity has completely changed the way I live my life, and who I live it with, so I encourage you to give it a whirl - if you feel aligned to, that is*(ish)*.

Appreciating The Little Things: My first proper walk with my family along the promenade at Cromer Beach, as the sun set during a warm evening in May 2024.

Epilogue - Ending in the middle

Well, this is the end.

Oh no it isn't!

That's true, I lied - it isn't.

OK, for this book it is definitely the end. But, as for my journey as a "fcuked up female-founder", I'm only in the middle, and I'm sure I have so many interesting people to meet, awesome opportunities to explore, and fun stuff yet to do.

Along the way, I've discovered that life as a founder of an impact-driven company is a whirlwind.

I can only compare my business journey to being a pilot of a Boeing 737 full of people, solely in charge of navigating them safely from "A" to "B".

During the flight, there's been turbulence, wind, rain, snow (and sometimes even earthquakes and tornados), causing the jumbo jet to thrash in all directions.

At times, the passengers have been in a frenzy, the cabin crew couldn't keep them calm, and oxygen masks popped out from the overhead compartments - leaving me flying the plane with one leg, while stretching the length of the aircraft, single-handedly placing every mask over every person's face.

Even though there were cabin crew on board to help me, and the passengers could have helped themselves, somehow all responsibility seemed to fall on my shoulders when the shit really hit the fan.

But, regardless of these times of immense pressure, I have always remained calm, stayed on task, and landed the plane without breaking a sweat. And, that same resilience, perseverance and dedication is what has shaped me into the accomplished leader I have become.

For years, I've felt pressured to fulfil the expectations of others, but I no longer bow to these pressures, and I find by ignoring the "worlds' definition" of success, I continue to strive towards my own definition of success. Backing this up with trusting my intuition, I don't chase the things that I have no interest in (i.e. I accumulate wealth to live a lifestyle that's stress-free and includes the people I love, doing things I enjoy - not to buy huge homes, fast cars, fancy holidays, or designer clothes and accessories!)

Encouraging the purchase of material items to portray success (and often getting into debt in the process), alongside "realism", are created by those in charge of "the system" in the attempt to control you to "follow rank" and "contribute to society" (focused on money). I won't allow myself to get sucked in and let these concepts stop me from achieving my ultimate "people-focused" goals.

I will continue to think bigger than I ever have before, in terms of what impact I can make, no longer holding myself back from my full potential (because I know that there's enough negative circumstances and devious people that will try to do that anyway). Plus, the more knowledge I gain, the more I will broaden my horizons (supported by advice from insightful books like *Dream, Create, Believe, Achieve* by one of my mentors, Darren Lewitt, and Dan Sullivan's *10x is easier than 2x*).

The only way is up, baby - and I'm already in flight!

The way I see it, we all enter this world in the same way, and we all exit it in the same way, so why not make the most of the time we have here, and chase our dreams no matter what?

However, even though *"feel the fear and do it anyway"* is a phrase that I really do agree with, I'd recommend taking care with what you let yourself get carried away with - because success often depends on timing and circumstances, so must be balanced with common sense and logic.

So, use both your heart and your head to make decisions (especially when it comes to making big "life altering" ones).

I'm still learning, and will never be "perfect" (if there is such a thing), but I know now that there's not a "one-size-fits-all approach" when it comes to business, career and life - so choosing what works for you with the information I have at the time is always the "best way".

My insight is to just let go and trust the process, and believe in the synchronicities that life presents to you (as Katie said in her Foreword) - knowing that things will naturally fall into place as they are meant to.

Ultimately, live your life by your own rules.

And, when you do face feelings of self-doubt or imposter syndrome (yes, unfortunately these will still happen from time to time - however, strong and confident we are feeling - as that's "human nature"), use your mind to take you to moments and places where you have felt pure joy, acceptance, and gratitude (for me, it's memories of holidays with my family, being outside in nature, and moments of fun with my children and dogs) and remind yourself of all the successes and learning experiences that have got you to where you are today.

Please remember that your mind is so powerful, and your perspective can change the way you see the world (and your place in it). If you are worried or struggling, then seek support or guidance, as a problem shared (with the right person) is often a problem halved.

As a business leader or career-climber, it's common to feel alone and isolated at times, so surrounding yourself with like-minded people that have your best interests at heart will give you the strength, drive and resilience to keep on pushing to make your dreams come true.

Most of all, the most valuable piece of wisdom I can pass on to you from my own journey is that if you're not at your best in terms of your mental health, physical health, nutrition, diet, sleep, etc, then your business or career isn't going to be at it's best either - and this will sabotage your chances of success (and likely affect the people around you, too). So, focus on looking after yourself first, and the rest will naturally fall into place (I promise).

If you are a woman on a growth journey like mine (or any gender identity really, as everything is fully inclusive and valuable!), and have professional aspirations for your career or business that you'd love to see come true, then head on over to ProspHER's website for free advice, guidance and resources to help you to make your goals happen much quicker. ProspHER also delivers some pretty incredible events, and has an online community learning platform for personal and professional development that is second to none (if I do say so myself!)

You can find it all at www.prospher.co.uk.

Before I go, I'd like to dedicate this book to all of those people that have stuck by me along my journey, those who I have loved and lost, those that have taught me powerful lessons, and those that have shaped my path in some way. Whatever influence you have had on me and my life, I'm forever grateful.

I owe a lot of my business journey to Sara Greenfield, who was the incredible woman who entrusted me with taking over the small local women's business networking group from her in 2015 - which has grown into what my company has become today. Unfortunately, Sara is somewhere brighter now, but I keep the star in the ProspHER logo as a tribute to her.

I'm so blessed to have some loyal friends and my beautiful family for support, who love me for me and have been there for me through thick and thin. Special thanks to my "school mums" (Marieanne, Kelly, Kerry and Heidi) and my "oldest friend" (Fred), plus my cousins (Leona, Shona, Becky, Charli and Kayla), my husband (Matthew), kids (Ella and Alfie), mum and dad (Lorraine and Tony), brother (Luke), mother and father-in-law (Adele and John) and doggies (Buddy and Belle).

I conclude in saying that - for them, myself, and everyone that it helps - I will continue to forge my legacy with "Passion, Purpose and Power".

Always striving to "ProspHER"*(ish)*.

Thanks for sticking with me 'til the "middle-end"!

Best wishes,
Serena ✦

My Whole World: Me with my husband Matthew, daughter Ella, son Alfie, and "sausages" Buddy and Belle, in July 2024 (in a rare photo when we are all looking and smiling in the right direction!)

Printed in Great Britain
by Amazon

47214014R00066